Chaplain[illegible]
Mission

Shaping Christian Presence and Ministry in Schools

Sarah Watson

Priest in the Church of England

GROVE BOOKS LIMITED

RIDLEY HALL RD CAMBRIDGE CB3 9HU

Contents

Acknowledgments

With grateful thanks to Ann Casson for generously allowing me to build on her excellent research in *Lessons in Spiritual Development*. I am also indebted to the schools and chaplains that I spoke with and visited. Thanks also go to my supervisors and supporters throughout the writing of this book and to Bluecoat Academy Nottingham for introducing me to school chaplaincy and shaping my vocation.

AADE

Anglican Association of Directors of Education

First Impression October 2020

ISSN 2041-0964

ISBN 978 1 78827 140 0

1 Mission and Church Schools

For over two hundred years schools have formed an important part of the ministry and mission of the Church of England.[1] This booklet explores how school chaplaincy can contribute to the church's continued ministry and mission in schools. It identifies key features of chaplaincy, reflects on three key aspects of it and considers the appropriateness of such mission. Although drawing on examples of practice in church schools, it is hoped it will be helpful for those considering implementing, developing or reviewing chaplaincy within their own school, whatever its context.

Why Consider Mission in Schools?

Church of England schools are viewed as central to the church's mission in the nation,[2] with a vision for schools to be both 'deeply Christian' and 'serve the common good.'[3] Such schools, in both primary and secondary phases, educate approximately one million children, enabling 'more direct engagement with children and their families than any other contact, including regular Sunday worship.'[4] They perhaps enable the church's greatest place of engagement with the community. As a result, arguably, school chaplains have the potential to minister to more young people than parish churches, making their contribution to the church's mission significant in all schools where the church seeks engagement.

In 'Growing Faith,' the House of Bishops stressed the importance of every aspect of the church's mission being viewed through the lens of its impact on children and young people, with the relationship between churches, schools and households being vital in enabling faith to develop.[5] It recognized that the connections made at primary level are often lost as pupils move to secondary school—it is perhaps here that chaplaincy can provide its most significant contribution.

What Does Mission in Schools Look Like?

In order to discuss *how* chaplaincy can contribute to mission in schools, it is important to ask *what* is meant by mission, as there is a broad spectrum of views. For example, for some mission means a narrow focus on evangelism, whilst for others it is simply seen in the context of serving others. Andrew

Wright appears to incorporate both of these views, stating that mission in schools should seek:

> ...first, to bring persons into an encounter with God—in a manner that...respects their freedom—and teach, baptize and nurture Christian converts; secondly to work for the common good by responding to human need, challenging oppression and injustice, and caring for the environment'[6]

This view of mission in schools is in line with that expressed in 'The Five Marks of Mission':

> - To proclaim the good news of the kingdom
> - To teach, baptize and nurture new believers
> - To respond to human need by loving service
> - To transform unjust structures of society, to challenge violence of every kind and pursue peace and reconciliation
> - To strive to safeguard the integrity of creation, and sustain and renew the life of the Earth.[7]

Such a view of mission is holistic in approach and avoids some of the narrower definitions which focus exclusively on verbal proclamation and a call to response. It is not, however, the only understanding of the church's role and it is important to recognize and consider the view of mission that is being applied within one's own specific context, as that will clearly impact on any chaplaincy role within it.

Questions to Consider

- How would you define mission?
- How might this impact on the shape of chaplaincy in your context and the challenges it might bring?
- Is there a difference between church and community schools in approaches to mission?
- What are the implications in your own context?

Perspectives from Research on School Chaplaincy

2

Research has highlighted some common threads as to how chaplaincy functions in schools and how it relates to mission.[8]

Context Is Key—
There is No 'One Size Fits All' Expression of Chaplaincy

The outworking of chaplaincy can look very different between schools, whilst chaplains can come from a wide range of backgrounds. Some chaplains are ordained, others lay; some employed (often, but not exclusively, also as teachers of RE), others are volunteers, or teams may include a combination of the two. It is vital to consider both the backgrounds of the individuals involved and the school context in determining the right shape of chaplaincy for each school, which may of course change and evolve over time.

The Importance of the Chaplain's Presence in School

Despite there being no consensus on which shape of chaplaincy can be automatically applied to a school, chaplaincy was almost universally viewed as an important way in which the Christian ethos was made visible. The chaplain's physical presence as a walking sacrament was seen as particularly important to this, described by one headteacher as being 'the human face of God.'

John Stott, however, argues that presence alone is not enough but should be a prelude to proclamation, alongside social involvement.[9] This view seems to encapsulate a more holistic view of mission resonating with the Five Marks. It is particularly important in a context where there will be people from other faiths and none, reinforcing Archbishop Justin's view that the gospel is good news for *all*, with listening at its heart.[10]

Gavin Wakefield puts forward a similar view that, in terms of ethics, it is only through presence and social involvement that we earn the right to speak.[11] A holistic view of mission involves much more than simply proclamation; indeed, it can be argued that presence *and* social involvement *is* mission. Presence and listening are significant factors in the building of trust and relationships. Therefore, the presence of the chaplain is the precursor that can enable other aspects of mission to take place.

What Do We Know about the Chaplain's Role and How This Relates to Mission?

Research demonstrates that a chaplain's time is most involved with the first three Marks of Mission, through pastoral care and leading the spiritual and liturgical life of the school. The table below examines how a chaplain's role functions as mission by aligning research findings with the Marks of Mission; however, it should be noted that categories are not mutually exclusive and the examples cited not exhaustive.

Marks of Mission	Research on School Chaplaincy
Proclaim the good news of the kingdom	Commend Christian faith in word and action, expressing where God is at work and supporting other faiths. *Example*: collective worship; development of spirituality and how the school ethos permeates school life.
Teach, baptize and nurture new believers	Leading the community's spiritual life through prayer and worship. Teaching about faith and nurturing those on a journey of faith. *Example*: collective worship; contributions to the curriculum (not just RE); extracurricular groups.
Respond to human need by loving service	Accompanying people's life journey, bringing Christian insights where appropriate and making God visible. *Example*: serving the community (staff, pupils and sometimes parents) by providing pastoral care.
Transform unjust structures of society, to challenge violence of every kind and pursue peace and reconciliation	Providing a prophetic voice through addressing issues of injustice; providing challenge. *Example*: holding the school accountable to its Christian ethos; supporting student groups addressing issues of injustice.
To strive to safeguard the integrity of creation, and sustain and renew the life of the Earth	Teaching on this issue, leading by example and having a voice on environmental issues within and beyond the school. *Example*: eco initiatives in school.

Such examples are not just an atomized series of tasks but present a more holistic view of mission by providing opportunities to encounter God, through responding to human need and working for the common good, helping chaplaincy to offer the good news for all.

Ways in Which Chaplaincy is Expressed

Although there can be no singular expression of chaplaincy, there are three main ways in which chaplaincy is often displayed within schools. These, however, are not mutually exclusive.

Pastoral care—alongside leading public worship and teaching, this is perhaps the classic way in which chaplaincy is expressed and is usually a key feature of any model of chaplaincy, with listening as one of the most important skills required. The relationship of the chaplain to wider pastoral systems in a school is an important consideration. Although there are great strengths in each area of pastoral care working together, there are also pitfalls if the chaplain is perceived as part of the hierarchy and its power dynamics.

Builder of ethos—enabling the Christian ethos and bringing appropriate challenge to maintain this. The chaplain can play an important leadership role in promoting development and monitoring of the school's vision. In Anglican and Methodist schools this focuses on the development, implementation and impact of a school vision that is both inclusive and distinctively Christian.[12] As well as supporting the school's vision, the incarnational aspect of chaplaincy also means that chaplains themselves can seek to build a distinct chaplaincy ethos within the school.

New ways of being church—providing opportunities for the school community to engage with Christian faith so that school becomes an expression of church for those who join in.[13] This raises issues of inclusivity, particularly where pupils' personal commitment to faith is minimal or the context is multi-faith, and also of continuity, when a member of the 'church' moves on from the school.

Questions to Consider

- In what ways do the terms the 'human face of God,' 'making Christian ethos visible' or being a 'walking sacrament' help reflect the role of chaplaincy within schools?
- How does the chaplain's physical presence and availability in school impact upon the expression of chaplaincy in your context?
- How could some of the challenges of inclusivity and continuity presented by the 'school as church' be overcome?

3 Reflections on Three Key Aspects of School Chaplaincy

This chapter draws on research into leading Christian ethos schools, as well as the author's own school visits and conversations with chaplains, to explore three key aspects of chaplaincy, namely: presence, core function and physical space.[14]

Presence

The chaplain's presence in school is paramount to the effectiveness of chaplaincy and encapsulates the idea of incarnational ministry, where the chaplain is a visible representation of Christ, or 'the human face of God.' This approach was seen in Jesus' ministry and mission when he encountered people where they were, such as the woman at the well (John 4) or Zacchaeus (Luke 19).

An observation of this in practice comes from the John Wallis Church of England Academy in Ashford. At the academy gate, the students were welcomed by the chaplain. A simple routine task, yet several staff pointed to this as a time and place where the Christian ethos of the academy was most visible. Listening to the chaplain as he joked, cajoled and wished each student well showed the depth of the relationship of trust and care. He indicated this was a part of his role he most enjoys: 'I love being on the gate because I love welcoming the students in the morning.'

The missional effect of the chaplain's presence is evident at John Wallis. The welcoming at the gate models Christian hospitality, builds relationships and highlights the accessibility of the chaplain. Students seek the chaplain out for prayer, sometimes in the chapel but often in corridors. These opportunistic episodes are made possible by the chaplain's presence. The impact of this regarding the chaplain's missional role is clearly seen by students and staff and generates comments on the positive place of compassion, forgiveness, prayer and unconditional love within school life.

The effectiveness of chaplains is evident in the way that they are often viewed as Christian role models, with mission expressed through providing a visible demonstration of what it means to live out faith. Here, proclamation is as much by action as it is in words. This is particularly important where the chaplain may be one of the only Christians many students will encounter. John Wallis' chaplain said:

> You yourself are the best Bible that some people will ever read. So, the way I am, the way I conduct myself, the way they see me behaving is probably the only Bible they might pick up...it's about mirroring the gospel values to them.

This was also evident in the St Mary Redcliffe and Temple School in Bristol, where the Christian ethos of the school is articulated through key values, including faith, made particularly identifiable through the work of chaplaincy. Sixth form students openly shared their experience of faith and how it impacted upon their lives, explaining how they were influenced by the way the chaplain modelled faith and leadership, especially through being a Christian presence, by offering and encouraging prayer, and in working with others.

Building respect and trust is a priority, which such presence facilitates. One chaplain explained how demonstrating a commitment to stay with the students and not let them down helps students to feel secure. This is viewed as pertinent in a context where students have low self-worth and parental support is not always evident. The chaplain can also be an ambassador for stability, resurrection and hope in challenging contexts and situations.

This emphasis on presence also extends to families with whom chaplains often sit, listening and reflecting. In some cases, there are home visits to new Year Seven students, taking food parcels to families in need or, where appropriate, facilitating support from other agencies.

The Ascension Trust, who developed the Street Pastors Scheme, have implemented another one called School Pastors, which is also based around presence and has many similarities to chaplaincy.[15] Pastors are usually volunteers from the local Christian community, rather than school employees, and spend time patrolling an area of the school, or even bus routes, engaging with students and helping to minimize incidents and bullying, which particularly resonates with the fourth Mark of Mission.

School pastors often offer additional pastoral support and may also get involved with clubs, mentoring or collective worship, thus extending the range of mission. Volunteers are provided with training including safeguarding, listening skills and conflict management. Their uniform gives them a highly visible presence in the school; their presence allows bridge building, listening and Christian role modelling. The advantage of using such volunteers is that some students may speak to them in a different way to how they would interact with paid members of staff who are seen as part of the establishment.

It is important to ask the question: what is the purpose of the chaplain's or school pastor's presence in school and how can it be categorized as *mission*? Response to human need through loving service and seeking peace and reconciliation seems to be the primary mode of mission, but this does not mean other aspects are absent. Leading worship and offering prayer, for example, add another dimension of mission evident in many schools.

It would also be easy to think that the significance attributed to presence meant that chaplaincy is done to others by the chaplain; however, in most expressions of chaplaincy, although the chaplain is pivotal, staff, local churches and students are also involved. For example, at Abbey Grange Church of England Academy in Leeds, chaplaincy is well co-ordinated by the chaplain, who enables students in particular to take a lead. The impact of this is that students come to believe that they can make a difference in the world and are active within the school and beyond.

Although the chaplain is pivotal, staff, local churches and students are also involved

However, the presence of a chaplain does not mean that they are the only one embodying the school's Christian ethos. Senior leadership and governors in particular have a significant role to play, in both embodying the ethos and supporting its expression throughout the school. For example, John Wallis students commented that it was possible to tell they were a Christian school because of how forgiveness was evident, or the way in which the principal prayed for people in the community.

It is also important to recognize that the personality and interests of the individual chaplain will inevitably impact upon the shape of what takes place. Presence cannot be divorced from the person.

Core Function

It is clear that chaplains play a significant role in the school's pastoral system, most reflective of the third Mark of Mission, and are often a key component in its Christian ethos, working alongside others who are involved in pastoral support, such as year leaders or mentors. Pastoral care appears to work best where chaplaincy has strong links to the pastoral team (including school counsellors), enabling referrals and signposting to the right service where appropriate. In a culture where issues related to mental health among young people are rising, chaplains can have a positive impact as providers of listening and support. However, within any pastoral role it is important to consider the training, confidentiality, trust and safeguarding implications.

The provision of pastoral care alone does not, by definition, make chaplaincy distinctively Christian. However, pastoral care can embody such values by the way in which mistakes are seen to be dealt with, for example. The Christian promotion of forgiveness, restoration, reconciliation and hope for the future can make a significant impact.

Alongside pastoral care the chaplain usually has a key role in the worship and teaching life of the school, including major festivals and events in the rhythm of a school year. This is most closely aligned with the first two Marks of Mission. Usually the pattern for daily worship and prayer is facilitated by the chaplain, which helps to embed the Christian ethos across the school. Confirmation and baptism also take place in some settings, as well as regular eucharistic services and celebrations at major festivals. Here the involvement of local churches is also often important and helps strengthen links between the school and the local church.

Developing student leadership is often a facet of the chaplain's role

In many schools, developing student leadership is often a facet of the chaplain's role, and is seen in areas such as student-led worship or Christian Unions. Here we particularly note the first and second Marks of Mission in action, which in turn may lead to other elements of mission being expressed, such as social action initiatives and fundraising. This is reflective of the role of leaders equipping others for works of service, as urged in Ephesians 4.

Outreach into the community and links with local churches can be another core function. This is seen, for example, in the John Wallis chaplain's visits to homes, or in the support offered by St Mary Redcliffe and Temple School Year Eight students to a weekly lunch club in the Methodist community centre adjacent to the school. Here the chaplain also works closely with the parish youth worker and other local agents, to run community events for families in the area.

Within all of this, the chaplain's interaction with the senior team and governors is important. Where there is a high level of trust, relationship and security, the chaplain is not only supported and resourced but also able to offer a supportive yet critical voice, holding the school to account in maintaining and developing its Christian ethos. The chaplain may also provide support and pastoral care to the head teacher in what can be a lonely role. The extent to which the chaplain participates in senior leadership and governors' meetings can vary from school to school and can bring both benefits and challenges.

In any discussion of what a chaplain does it is important to recognize what has been called the 'culture of chaos' in schools. Allowing for God in the interruptions is a key component of school chaplaincy, which is by nature somewhat unpredictable, organic and spontaneous.

Physical Space

In many schools a physical space serves as a focal point and a visible sign of chaplaincy. The space may vary in size and capacity, from a small office to a large chapel. The advantage of such dedicated space is that chaplaincy is identifiable and embodied in both person and place. Hence the physical space can become a safe place where the services of chaplaincy can be accessed.

An example of this is the St Mary Redcliffe and Temple School, where a conscious decision has been made to have a chaplaincy room situated just off the main canteen, a central location which clearly helps facilitate the work of chaplaincy. Room 91 is named after the psalm, denoting a place of refuge, an accessible safe space where the chaplain, the 'human face of God,' can be easily sought. The room contains the chaplain's desk, sofas, a focus for worship, artwork and table football. It is primarily a place where students come for pastoral care and to gain support in planning clubs. The impact of this is that it is viewed by students as a place where they are able to come to talk and share ideas, in an environment which is welcoming and accepting of them regardless of beliefs or where they are in their journey of faith.

The size of the room or chapel will impact upon how it is used. For example, Room 91 holds around fifteen people, therefore only small groups—including staff prayers and Lent eucharists—can take place there. Many larger activities, including collective worship and most clubs, are held in other locations such as the hall, classrooms or the sixth form's multi-use room. The school also holds regular services in the parish church, strengthening links and enabling the school community to come together.

Abbey Grange provides a different example of how physical space is utilized. Here there is a bigger space, a chapel which can hold a tutor group and which acts as a chaplaincy hub. The chaplain also has a separate office where people can find her, but it is not the central place for chaplaincy. As well as hosting class-sized groups, the chapel also provides space for those who seek quiet, and becomes a worship space at different times of the day. Whilst most activities take place here, during a visit to the school the chaplain was observed hosting a mindfulness group in a classroom, whilst Year Ten students led a Year Seven small group in the chapel.

A physical space can become the focal point for chaplaincy

A physical space can become the focal point for chaplaincy, with some activities taking place in the space and others planned within its walls, to be taken out into the school or community. Examples of this include the St Mary Redcliffe and Temple School supporting links with a Ugandan school through prayer, visits and hospitality during return trips. Another example comes from Abbey Grange and its array of student-led fundraising activities and initiatives, such as Fairtrade or the Global Justice Group.

The existence of a physical space does not automatically guarantee that mission is taking place. It is possible for a venue to become inward looking and so become a limiting factor. It is therefore important to consider how space may facilitate the actual outreach work of chaplaincy, as well as how it is visible and accessible. Used well, it can become a central point for missional expression with activities taking place both within and beyond the base. For example, worship, prayer, Christian nurture or pastoral care often take place within the space, in keeping with the first three Marks of Mission. However, many activities are planned within the base and spin out from it. Together these often encompass most exemplars of the Marks of Mission, from Christian groups and worship to ecological activities, response to human need and seeking transformation in society. This was particularly evident at Abbey Grange and was reflected on the walls of the chapel, which display many posters advertising charity events, social justice initiatives, artwork, photos and prayers penned on Post-it notes, addressing personal, local and global issues.

The availability of a dedicated room does not automatically result in a successful expression of chaplaincy. Where there is a physical space both the person and the place are significant in enhancing the effectiveness of chaplaincy in the school. However, its lack may constitute a challenge for pastoral support in particular, as a dedicated chaplaincy room or chapel can often provide a focal point in times of crisis. The further advantage of such a physical space is that it accommodates resources and groups and is a central, identifiable place for meetings and activities.

The location of a room is also important, impacting upon its profile and accessibility. What is considered as the best site for a base will vary according to school architecture and context, but visibility in a central location would certainly help people to access that space and therefore enhance its effectiveness.

A holistic expression of mission can emerge where these different aspects of chaplaincy come together, alongside other facets of the school's Christian ethos. Here proclamation in word and action, including social action, sits alongside nurture, discipleship and loving service.

Questions to Consider

- How could chaplaincy as presence be expressed within your context?
- What functions of chaplaincy are evident in your context?
  - ◊ What could be further developed, taking into consideration personnel, time and place?

- Is there a space that can be made available in your school?
    - ◊ If so, how can it be utilized?
    - ◊ If not, how can chaplaincy be alternatively resourced and developed?

Implications for Chaplaincy in Schools

4

Having explored different aspects and expressions of chaplaincy, this chapter examines some of the key considerations which impact on how chaplaincy contributes to a school.

Christian Ethos

One of the ways in which school chaplaincy differs from other expressions of chaplaincy is that it is often an integral part of the institution and its ethos, especially in church schools, but also in secular contexts where chaplains are employed. In *A Theology for Chaplaincy,* Rowan Clare Williams speaks of chaplaincy in secular institutions as, 'learning to sing the Lord's song in a strange land where the story, which is central to us, is unfamiliar to those we serve.'[16] Whilst her observations might be true for chaplaincy in non-church schools, the picture is a little different in church schools. Here, it is arguable that chaplains are not 'singing the Lord's song in a strange land,' as they clearly operate within a Christian framework.

However, where chaplaincy is taking place in a Church of England school, the historic remit of such schools is to serve the whole community, regardless of faith, with a focus on education for—and service to—all. Therefore, although the context of a church school provides a Christian ethos (which is more explicit in some schools than others), it might also be true that the song being sung is unfamiliar to many within each school who come from another faith background, or none.

Where chaplaincy takes place in a context where the Christian ethos *is* explicit, even if all its stakeholders are not Christian, it differs from the secular environment of a non-church school where there will be strict parameters around any suggestion of evangelism. There, chaplaincy might have a role in contributing to the wider ethos, but any mission is far more aligned to the third, and sometimes fourth, Mark of Mission. By way of contrast, in church schools, chaplaincy may exemplify the school's foundation through proclamation and Christian teaching, via collective worship or extracurricular groups for example.

Sacred Space and Other Faiths

The role of sacred space can also differ in a church school if there is an area set aside for chaplaincy. Many chaplains in secular environments do not have a dedicated space, whilst others, such as in hospitals and airports, may have a sacred venue which is multi-faith. Some schools have a multi-faith room which may include, or be distinct from, a chapel or chaplaincy room. As highlighted in the previous chapter, regardless of the provision of a sacred space, finding locations and times for pastoral conversations where students are likely to engage is an important consideration.

Where people of other faiths or none are present, chaplaincy should operate with respect for, and dialogue with, all, recognizing that in any activity that could be deemed missional, autonomy in expression of faith is important. This raises questions about the role of the chaplain in supporting those of another faith and the provision, for example, of a prayer space. This can be a matter of debate and raises some interesting theological questions, as well as discussions about the remit of the team, which are worthy of consideration.

Parental Choice

Church schools are often popular with parents, including those from other faiths. The reasons for parents choosing a church school, when a choice is available, are often educational but could include the ethos and role of faith, which can vary between contexts.[17] This raises questions about parental buy in to the Christian ethos of church schools in particular, and whether this makes a difference to the expression of chaplaincy and the appropriateness of any missional activity.

How the Institution Understands Chaplaincy

As well as parental perception, how chaplaincy is received or understood by the institution is also key. Leadership has a vital role in setting the tone in any school, and this cannot be understated.[18] Chaplaincy appears to work best where it is endorsed, supported and profiled by senior management and governors. When this happens (as in the schools exemplified in this book), it provides another way in which the Christian ethos becomes embodied in church schools, rather than simply being words on a wall or website!

The time and role description allocated to chaplaincy, as well as the provision of a physical space, have a significant impact upon its shape and effectiveness, as has been evident in the schools observed. The close involvement of the local parish and other churches can be an asset both for the school and local churches. This is not exclusive to church schools and can work well in secular school contexts too.

It is also important to recognize that, although significant, it is not the responsibility of the chaplaincy team to carry the *whole* Christian ethos of a church school, and this must be clearly recognized and understood within the school. The responsibility for ethos lies with the leadership team and governors, those who design and deliver the curriculum, and with the wider pastoral team. Many good examples of practice are described in the research on leading Christian ethos schools referenced in chapter three. The SIAMS framework for Church of England schools also seeks to ensure that the Christian ethos runs through the whole of school life, with chaplaincy playing its part where it is present.

Questions to Consider

- In what ways does the school's ethos, alongside its demographic and the ability of parents to choose the school, impact on the shape of chaplaincy in your context?
- How does the vision and support of senior leadership and governors impact upon chaplaincy in your context?

  ◊ How could this be strengthened or developed?

5 Some Theological and Ethical Questions

Having discussed the important place church schools have within the mission of the church and the role that chaplaincy can play within them, the following chapter considers some ensuing theological and ethical questions.

Is Mission Appropriate in Church Schools?

It could be argued that mission within a school, whose primary purpose is to provide education—not to fill pews—has the potential to be exploitative. The Church of England Education Office states that its schools should be both deeply Christian and serve the common good, therefore any expression of chaplaincy in church schools should reflect this by serving the whole community regardless of commitment to faith.[19]

It is important to recognize that education (as the primary purpose of schools) in itself can be missional, through loving service and tackling unjust structures in society. This is particularly evident in places of deprivation and is in the DNA of most Church of England schools. This reflects a more holistic view of mission, rather than it being defined solely as evangelism. Here the gospel is seen as good news for all: it includes pursuit of the common good regardless of commitment to faith, working towards 'life in all its fullness' rather than simply forgiveness of sins and the promise of eternal life (John 10.10). A holistic approach provides opportunities for mission and encountering faith without compulsion; it values the individual and encourages human flourishing for all, regardless of faith.

Ethical Mission

Many Christians view mission as a fundamental part of Christianity and, where the Christian ethos is explicit in a church school, telling the Christian story is often viewed as part of the narrative of such schools. However, any missional activity must be conducted in an ethical manner and without compulsion, which is particularly pertinent when we consider the first two Marks of Mission.[20]

Is it possible for school chaplaincy to provide a ministry which enables human flourishing and working for the common good, with respect for those of other faiths and none, alongside providing opportunities to explore and encounter Christian faith? If so, how does this take place without compulsion or expectation of Christian commitment, where faith is offered but never imposed and which values an individual's worth, dignity and autonomy?

The appropriateness and place of the first two Marks of Mission within a school context is a matter of debate and needs careful consideration. It could be argued that in sending their child to a church school parents/carers accept or even expect that there will be some proclamation and teaching of Christian faith, for example in collective worship and RE. However, it could also be argued that the chaplain should be more of a listener and servant than a preacher. Where faith is shared, it must be done sensitively and respectfully, without compulsion.

Power Dynamics

Another consideration is the potential power dynamic between adults and students within a school, where adults often are seen to represent authority. The age and stage of development of the child need careful consideration. This is particularly important when working with vulnerable children, where the well-being of the whole child and safeguarding considerations are paramount.

Alongside this is the consideration that in some settings, such as collective worship, students are a captive audience. This situation is different from talking with somebody on the street, in a church context or in a different sector of chaplaincy. In school contexts the element of choice about being present is not available, unless parents opt to withdraw their child from the school or more specifically from collective worship and/or RE. For those present, including staff, there should be no compulsion or expectation of response and, where possible, choice given, for example when praying, or at a school eucharist.

Related to this there will be the strengths and weaknesses of the individual chaplain, whether they are ordained or lay, paid or volunteer, teacher or non-teacher. Students might be more willing to talk with someone they do not associate as being part of the school staff; however, if volunteers come in only occasionally, relationships might not be built sufficiently. There is also the danger that chaplains could be viewed with suspicion by some students—in one context, a chaplain was asked about being 'a spy for the teachers'! There will be merits and pitfalls in each approach, yet it is important to consider these concerns when shaping an expression of chaplaincy for a particular school. There is no perfect expression of chaplaincy; there are pros and cons for each. However, an awareness of potential issues is a helpful place from which to start appropriate discussions.

There is no perfect expression of chaplaincy

Multi-faith Context

Many church schools are situated in a multi-faith context. Many of their students will enter and leave the school adhering to their particular religion. However, mutual understanding of faith, where people are listened to with respect and humility despite differences, aids mutual understanding and helps enable societal cohesion. This, arguably, is a component of mission, in seeking to pursue reconciliation and peace in society.

The extent of support for other faiths can be contentious and raises theological and practical questions. Should the chaplain support other faiths in their worship, and is this appropriate or even desirable? Should there be provision of prayer spaces for other faiths? Diane Tregale recognizes the importance of supporting people of other faiths but states that in the Church of England school context, 'Chaplaincy must be specifically Christian if it is to fulfil the mission of the church.'[21] This, however, could well be a matter of debate.

Parental Understanding

Parental understanding of the school's ethos is an important factor and is where chaplaincy in church schools differs in some regards from a secular environment. Hopefully there is an understanding that the Christian ethos is an important feature of school life. Nonetheless it must be undertaken ethically and sensitively. As raised previously, although in theory all parents have a choice whether to send their child to a church school, for some it might be the only school in the area. Does this impact upon perceived permission for Christian activity or mission?

Ecclesiological Questions and Relation to the Local Church

As well as ethical and theological issues, there are ecclesiological questions, particularly in relation to the second Mark of Mission. Which elements of teaching and nurture are appropriate in school, what is age-related and what is more the province of the local church? For example, is it the school's role to point those wanting baptism or confirmation to the local church or is it appropriate for these rites to take place within a school context? In practice, baptisms rarely take place in schools but eucharist services and, sometimes, confirmations are more common.

How does / can the chaplaincy team and local church work together? It is important to recognize that if the chaplaincy team is ecumenical, there are likely to be denominational and theological differences which need consideration, for example around baptism, confirmation and holy communion. It is important that a sense of mutual flourishing is fostered, taking into account the diversity within Christianity, alongside an appreciation for—and respect of—the school's denominational identity (where that is a factor). There also needs to be sensitivity surrounding ethical issues, especially where the theological position of an individual chaplain might differ from the equality policy of the institution. Where this is the case, the chaplain is obliged to follow the school's policies if they are to operate within that school. Therefore, training which includes school policies and procedures is essential in clarifying expectations.

Can a School be a Church?

The school environment could be the only place where students are able to worship and explore faith. Does the school therefore become their church? How do the age of a child and developmental stage of the individual impact on this? If school equates to church, what happens to students or staff and their Christian journey when they leave that school? How does the concept work in a Church of England school operating under the parish system? Who has the pastoral responsibility and the cure of souls? What about those in school who may also be part of another church, denomination or faith? There are many questions and issues that the concept of the school as church raises.

It could be helpful for chaplains to take a long-term view: one of sowing seeds, with a recognition that when people leave the school, it is not the end of the story. The influence of chaplaincy on an individual's life might never be known or measured by those involved in chaplaincy, which is indeed true of all those engaged in education.

Questions to Consider

- Does chaplaincy in church schools have to be exclusively Christian to fulfil the church's mission?

  ◊ What might this look like in your context?

- What are the power dynamics in your situation?

  ◊ How can any abuse of power be safeguarded against?

- Which of the issues raised above are most relevant to your context?

  ◊ How might these issues be addressed?

6 What About 'My' School?

When thinking about chaplaincy and how it can contribute to mission within schools, it is essential to consider context, people, profile and role.

Context is Key

In any contextual mission an understanding of that context is paramount, and schools are no different. What is clear is that, in taking context seriously, school chaplaincy cannot be a one-size-fits-all phenomenon. What works and is an appropriate expression of chaplaincy and mission in one school might differ from another. It is therefore important to consider how chaplaincy has functioned historically in a given school and how this fits with the current context. This might have changed from when chaplaincy was introduced due to societal or other shifts, including the school's personnel and demographic.

Where the context is a Church of England school, any expression of chaplaincy as mission should seek to be in line with the vision for education, *Deeply Christian, Serving the Common Good*, which is both faithfully Christian and promotes education for the good of the whole community, aiming to draw out a person's potential and enable human flourishing, regardless of their faith.[22] Consideration of how pursuit of the common good can go alongside being deeply Christian in this context is essential.

When thinking about how chaplaincy contributes to mission, many contextual factors need noting, including the relationship with, and involvement of, the local parish and other churches. The extent and function of missional chaplaincy will also be influenced by funding, the vision of governors and senior leadership, as well as the school's ethos, demographic, history, tradition and the students' age and stage of development. Other determining factors include what is available in terms of space, time and resources, alongside the personality and skills of the chaplain and/or chaplaincy team. Accommodating these factors will result in more effective mission than simply trying to transpose an expression of chaplaincy from one context to another.

People are Key

What are the attributes of the chaplain, their character and church tradition? These are worth noting, as is the vision of the person/group who sets the agenda and appoints the chaplain, since all these factors might determine the shape of chaplaincy and consequently its contribution to mission. Securing a chaplain with time, commitment and vision—plus clear leadership by the school's governors and senior leaders—are required to work out an effective expression of chaplaincy within the school.

Should there be a single chaplain or a team? A team approach gets away from the 'lonely outpost' expression of one-person chaplaincy and can draw in a variety of strengths, skills, gifts and passions to supplement those of the chaplain, thus forming a complementary team. When Jesus sent people out into mission it was within such teams, whilst the *Public Face of God* concluded that, in chaplaincy, 'teamwork is crucial,' noting that 'chaplaincy is most successful when shared with others who are supportive and prayerful.'[23] If combined with appropriate leadership and oversight, a combination of volunteers and a full-time chaplain can be effective, facilitating involvement with both individuals and groups.

Creating a chaplaincy team which incorporates a range of denominations, and is representative of the specific context, is also helpful. A mixture of age and gender may strengthen a team—for example, using youth workers, teachers and sixth form prefects as well as older people who can be grandparent-like figures. Alongside this, considerations regarding diversity and inclusion are also important, particularly in representing the demographic context of the school.

Chaplaincy teams provide opportunities to think creatively

Chaplaincy teams provide opportunities to think creatively, such as having two part-time chaplains, or a team of volunteers with a co-ordinating chaplain. There is a need for flexibility, both in terms of personnel and resources; however, there does seem to be a direct correlation between the scope of chaplaincy as mission in a school and the time given to any substantive role.

Chaplaincy is often most missionally effective when relationships are formed. This takes time and explains why the character, presence and allocated hours of the chaplain will inevitably impact upon the scope and effectiveness of chaplaincy. This is especially true when working with those who often need to feel safe with an adult before talking deeply with them. That said, chaplaincy can still be effective even where time is limited, as long as the role and function of the chaplain is clearly thought through.

It is important to be realistic and to work with the resources available. If time is limited that does not mean that chaplaincy cannot be successful as mission. It is better to be effective within a smaller remit than to be over-ambitious. A chaplain who is available a few hours a week, for example, could restrict their role to leading collective worship, occasional events and offering designated time where they are available for pastoral care. It is important to guard against the danger of over-stretching chaplains, especially volunteers, who might become demotivated under pressure and give up the role.

Thought needs to be given to the employment status of a chaplain and, if formally employed, by whom. There are pros and cons of different approaches; however, if the chaplain is employed by the school, line management and appraisal implications must be considered. These could significantly influence the ability of the chaplain to be a critical friend, a particular requirement of the fourth Mark of Mission, challenging injustice and holding the school to account in relation to its ethos.

Even where the chaplain is employed elsewhere or is a volunteer, the power dynamic with senior leadership still needs to be thought through and will impact on the reach of chaplaincy and how it functions. It might be helpful if a local church or the diocese is involved in appointing, and / or subsequently appraising, the role. In some schools there might be a joint appointment between school and diocese, with both contributing financially to the post but with the line manager and appraiser being from outside the school's management structure.

Another consideration is succession management, given that key personnel may change, including the chaplain / chaplaincy team or senior leadership. Different people will bring different skills and passions to the table and the shape of chaplaincy will inevitably alter. However, if the school has a particular vision of how chaplaincy will function, and certain aspects of mission are deemed particularly relevant or important, it is imperative that these are clearly communicated in any appointment process.

The training of chaplains is essential

As well as selecting the right people, the training of chaplains is essential, particularly when a chaplain is new to the role. This must involve safeguarding (including DBS checks), health and safety, listening skills and grounding in the pastoral system. There should be an emphasis on ethics rather than proselytizing, so that questions about faith are responded to sensitively and appropriately. Training also needs to include the school's behaviour and other policies, such as where to find support if a behavioural or first aid issue arises. The training given by the Ascension Trust for Street and School Pastors provides some good examples.[24] Ongoing training, alongside regular meetings for team support, dialogue and evaluation, is essential.

Profile is Key

As we have seen, chaplaincy comes in all sorts of shapes and sizes. A key question is how chaplaincy is made visible and how that can impact on the effectiveness of mission. This involves both person and place: the time and availability of the chaplain, plus the provision and location of any physical space will significantly impact upon this.

The support given to chaplaincy is critical in terms of its profile. As highlighted previously, the role of senior leadership and governors in setting and supporting the school's vision—as well as establishing, resourcing and developing chaplaincy—cannot be understated. The local church and diocese can also play significant roles in upholding and promoting chaplaincy in schools. The key stakeholders and decision makers must consider and make provision for how chaplaincy is present and profiled in person and in place. These decisions, and the degree of ongoing support, will be determining factors in the shape, success and scope of chaplaincy and its contribution to mission in schools.

Where there is a physical space, its use depends on its availability according to—the school's demands and whether it is to be used exclusively for chaplaincy, usually a decision made by senior leaders. The visibility of the chaplain's presence in going to students, alongside provision of a physical venue they can come to, can be very effective, particularly when thought has been given to the space's layout. For example, comfortable chairs or a dedicated prayer area could help it to be more inviting and look less like a classroom.

The visibility of the chaplain's presence can be very effective

It is also helpful to consider under what name a chaplaincy operates and how that enables understanding of the role. In a diverse context where many students are not familiar with the term 'chaplain,' 'pastor' may be an alternative. Whatever name is adopted, it is likely to bring associations with it which could be either positive or negative. It is therefore important to communicate what the name means and the role of chaplaincy within the school. If there is a new chaplain or team, commissioning may also raise the profile of this ministry and give a sense of authorization for its work.

Another consideration when thinking about visibility is the uniform of the chaplain. An ordained chaplain in a clerical collar is clearly visible, but a chaplain's uniform—such as those worn by school pastors—or a chaplaincy lanyard can be helpful in identifying who chaplains are and making their presence more explicit, which can aid mission. There are also safeguarding implications in being able to clearly identify chaplains, and this ready recognition can facilitate accessibility and building of trust.

However, raising the profile of chaplaincy is not just a one-off event, the wearing of a uniform or a sign over a door, but is ongoing. Apart from the hours and space allocated to chaplaincy there are other ways of raising the profile of the role. For example, visibility on the school website, presence at parents' evenings and a role in key events—such as open days or speech nights—all play their part.

Role is Key

In devising or reimagining an expression of chaplaincy for a particular context, it is a helpful exercise to relate the Marks of Mission to what is appropriate. This will to some extent be shaped by the considerations above; however, some suggestions are included in the table below, which might or might not come under the remit of chaplaincy in each specific context.

Marks of Mission	Examples
To proclaim the good news of the kingdom	Collective worship, eucharist, *Alpha*, special events. (Note: consider non-verbal as well as verbal acts of proclamation)
To teach, baptize and nurture new believers	Collective worship, curriculum involvement, Christian Union, sacraments, confirmation
To respond to human need by loving service	Pastoral support, help with bereavement, mental well-being, bullying etc; links to pastoral team, charity work, serving at school events
To transform unjust structures of society, to challenge violence of every kind and pursue peace and reconciliation	Charity work and overseas mission trips, challenging injustices in the school structure.
To strive to safeguard the integrity of creation, and sustain and renew the life of the Earth	Curriculum involvement, extracurricular clubs, eg running a school allotment; living by example, eg turning lights off, picking up litter, using reusable bottles.

Unless chaplaincy is being introduced into a school for the first time or a new expression is being created, it is more about evolution than revolution. By nature, contextual mission is often experimental and organic rather than static.[25] Listening to the context, seeking where God is at work and joining in is key. Whilst constant change can be wearing, allowing for evaluation and reshaping within a framework is vital to ensure chaplaincy is appropriate and relevant.

School chaplaincy has much to contribute to the church's ongoing ministry and mission and can play a significant part in the development of any school community. Considering every individual context and the missional opportunities of chaplaincy therein raises important issues, which are well worth exploring and developing.

Questions to Consider

- Which Marks of Mission are most relevant for my context?
  ◊ How may they be expressed?
- How can chaplaincy in my context be both 'deeply Christian' and 'serve the common good'?
- What are the key considerations of context, people, profile and role in my school?
  ◊ How will these impact on the expression of chaplaincy?
- Is some kind of chaplaincy uniform helpful? If so, what?
  ◊ What are the advantages and disadvantages of this?

Notes

1 H Worsley (ed), *Anglican Church School Education: Moving Beyond the First Two Hundred Years* (London: Bloomsbury Academic, 2014).

2 R Dearing, *The Way Ahead: Church of England Schools in the New Millennium* (London: Church House Publishing, 2001) p 10.

3 Church of England, *Church of England Vision for Education: Deeply Christian, Serving the Common Good* (London: Church House Publishing, 2016).

4 P Chadwick, *Church Schools of the Future—Review* (London: Archbishops' Council Education Division, 2012) p 3.

5 D Clinton, N Genders and D Male, 'Growing Faith: Churches, Schools and Households' GS2121 (London: General Synod of the Church of England, 2019).

6 A Wright, 'Church School Ministry as Contextual Theology,' in H Worsley (ed), *Anglican Church School Education: Moving Beyond the First Two Hundred Years* (London: Bloomsbury Academic, 2014) pp 186–206.

7 Anglican Communion, 'Marks of Mission,' 1984. Accessed 13 October 2020: https://www.anglicancommunion.org/mission/marks-of-mission.aspx.

8 See for example: M Camp, *The Public Face of God, Chaplaincy in Anglican Secondary Schools and Academies in England and Wales* (London: Church of England Archbishops Council Education Division, 2014); J Caperon, 'School Chaplaincy: What Does Research Tell Us?' The Bloxham Project, *Project Papers* 45 (Oxford: The Bloxham Project, 2011); A Casson, T Cooling and L Francis, *Lessons in Spiritual Development* (London: Church House Publishing, 2017); D Tregale, *Fresh Experiences of School Chaplaincy* (Grove Education booklet eD6).

9 J Stott (ed), *Making Christ Known: Historic Mission Documents from the Lausanne Movement, 1974–1989* (Carlisle: Paternoster Press, 1996) pp 20, 26.

10 J Welby, 'Archbishop Justin Welby's Deo Gloria Trust lecture on evangelism and other faiths,' 2019. Accessed 13 October 2020: www.archbishopofcanterbury.org/speaking-and-writing/speeches/archbishop-justin-welbys-deo-gloria-trust-lecture-evangelism-and

11 G Wakefield, *Doing Evangelism Ethically* (Grove Evangelism booklet Ev108) p 24.

12 The Church of England Education Office and The Methodist Church, *Statutory Inspection of Anglican and Methodist Schools* (London: Church House Publishing, 2018) p 2.

13 D Tregale, *op cit*.

14 A Casson, T Cooling, and L Francis, *op cit*.

15 Ascension Trust (homepage), n.d. Accessed 13 October 2020: www.ascensiontrust.org.uk

16 R C Williams, *A Theology for Chaplaincy* (Grove Education booklet eD34).

17 G Davie, *Religion in Britain Since 1945: Believing without Belonging (Making Contemporary Britain)* (Cambridge, MA: Blackwell Publishers, 1994) pp 128–130, 134; and see also FAIRUK, *British Muslims and Education* (Surrey: Open Society Institute, 2005) p 122.

18 A Casson, T Cooling and L Francis, *op cit*, p 6.

19 Church of England, *Church of England Vision for Education: Deeply Christian, Serving the Common Good*, *op cit*.

20 Wakefield, *op cit*, pp 5–25.

21 Tregale, *op cit*, p 14.

22 Church of England, *Church of England Vision for Education: Deeply Christian, Serving the Common Good*, *op cit*.

23 Camp, *op cit*, pp 8–23.

24 School Pastors (homepage), n.d. Accessed 13 October 2020: https://www.schoolpastors.org.uk

25 D Bosch, *Transforming Mission: Paradigm Shifts in Theology of Mission* (New York: Orbis Books, 1991) p 437.